OXYTOCIN

The Hormone of Healing and Hope

Paul Zak, PhD, FACSM

Copyright © 2012 K Paul Stoller. All rights reserved. No part of this book may be reproduced in any manner whatsoever without written permission except in the case of brief quotations embodied in critical articles and reviews. For information, write to:

Dream Treader Press
www.dreamtreaderpress.com

Manufactured in the United States of America

10 9 8 7 6 5 4 3 2 1

Edited by Debra Evans
Book Design by Anthony J.W. Benson & Anthony Sclavi

Contents

Introduction 1

Part I 5
Oxytocin – An Overview

Part II 9
Oxytocin and Its Impact on the Maladies of Our Time

Part III 17
Oxytocin – Sources and Dosage

Conclusion 21

Hope for the Future 24

About K Paul Stoller, MD, FACHM 27

Introduction

How a Hormone Saved Me...*and what it can do for you*

This little ebook may be among the most important books you will ever have in your personal library. However, I make this bold statement not because I'm the author, but because it brings to light the extraordinarily beneficial uses of the hormone called oxytocin. Oxytocin is also accurately described as a neuropeptide, and it's produced in both women and men. Although it's often associated with female reproduction, more recently oxytocin has become known as "the love hormone" as it brings forth feelings of trust, security, connection, calmness, and contentment.

As a doctor, I first came to learn about oxytocin in my work with brain-injured patients where it was used to mitigate the anxiety issues they often contend with. My primary focus was using oxytocin with children living with cerebral palsy, as well as environmental encephalitic syndrome (which is erroneously called autism in most cases and will be briefly addressed in the pages ahead).

Over time, I have come to discover the profound potential for healing that oxytocin offers related to many of the great ailments of our time—including mental illness, addictions, sexual dysfunction, cancer, and grief.

My knowledge of using oxytocin in the treatment of grief is first-hand. In 2007, my beloved 16-year old son Galen was killed in a train accident, sending me into a chasm of what I came to view as pathological grief—where I was unable to modulate obsessive thoughts about how my son died, what he might have experienced, what if I had been able to be there, and so on. This collection of fear, anxiety, and panic took on a life of its own, as if it were a separate thought-stream that I had no control of. It was suffocating and debilitating.

Although I had become adept at using oxytocin for treating fear and anxiety in children on the autism spectrum, it took me over three weeks after my son passed until I had the idea that it might help me too. I was so far down the rabbit hole of grief that I could feel a circadian miasm, of sorts. Let me explain. There are periods each day—the hour before sun-up and the hour after sundown—that the ancients acknowledged as being especially potent times. They referred to the hour before sunrise as "the hour of the wolf" and the hour after sunset as the bewitching hour. On mornings when I was sleeping during that pre-dawn period (the hour of the wolf), I would have the most distressing and horrible nightmares. When someone is already in a state of distress — panic and fear can be greatly intensified in these hours.

Once I finally had the epiphany that I should try oxytocin on myself, I waited until I was under the influence of one of these unpleasant miasmas and then began my experiment. One night, I set my alarm to wake up before this period and dosed myself with oxytocin, and the outcome felt nearly miraculous. The severity of obsessive negative thoughts during this acute grieving period was altered within minutes after the application of an oxytocin nasal spray. Whereas before I had to breathe through this emotionally difficult hour as if I were in a Lamaze class, that survival strategy became unnecessary with the use of oxytocin. This time, I was actually able to play music until the sun came up.

It took about ten minutes to experience the full effect, and with each passing minute a great sense of emotional equanimity took place. The panic and fear dropped away from me as if I were shedding clothing. If I wanted to think about my son's train accident, I could. But the moment I didn't want to think about it, the accident faded into the background of my mind. It wasn't there hammering away at me as if it had a life of its own. By successfully diverting these negative feelings from wherever they would have taken me, I was able to process my grief without the interference of negative obsessions. This was invaluable, to say the very least, and kept me from developing severe post-traumatic stress disorder (PTSD)…because that was certainly where I was headed.

Forty-five days after my son passed in 2007, I was giving a lecture at the MIND Institute at the University of California at Davis about how hyperbaric oxygen therapy can influence damaged neurons in the brains of autistic children. In private, I met with Dr. Robert Hendren, then the head of the MIND Institute before leaving to Chair the Child Psychiatry department at UCSF. After talking with him about my work with autistic children and oxytocin, I then told Dr. Hendren of the relief I had found from my grief and the website I had established for others needing help out of the quicksand of despair – www.GriefSOS.com. Interestingly, in 2009 the MIND Institute invited Dr. Eric Hollander, Chair Child Psychiatry, Mount Sinai School of Medicine to lecture on the use of oxytocin in those diagnosed with autism (the lecture is viewable in its entirety on YouTube[1]).

To date, I have never prescribed oxytocin for a patient in grief who did not report significant benefit from its use. As for myself, after just a few weeks I was able to completely stop using oxytocin. In that short period of time, it gave me the ability to deal with the worst kind of emotional pain without getting completely swallowed up by it.

Over the past several years, I have had a growing sense of urgency to inform other doctors and healthcare practitioners about the untapped potential of using oxytocin as part of a

---

[1] http://www.youtube.com/watch?v=BEAgT91XV5A&feature=related

standard approach to treating those in grief, and especially parents who have lost a child.

Just as importantly, it's time for this miraculous hormone to become widely known and generally understood by people outside of the medical field. Toward that end, I have intentionally written this ebook as an overview of oxytocin, using as few words as possible to illuminate its benefits without getting overly technical. Rather than aiming to be a comprehensive thesis on oxytocin, this book is expressly written as a concise introduction with solid medical science behind it. At the heart of the matter, I want those who need oxytocin to have the information they need, to be empowered to ask for it, and to have a solid rationale behind their request.

My promise to you, the reader, is to convey the important details about oxytocin while not weighing your reading experience down with too many terms that are better off in a biology textbook or classroom. You see, although oxytocin can support your physical health in a myriad of ways, I'm interested in your total wellness—body, mind, and soul. And my goal is to give you access to information that will support the well-being of you and your loved ones without delay.

So let's start at the beginning.

Part I

Oxytocin – An Overview

How is oxytocin made?

Oxytocin is a hormone manufactured in the hypothalamus, the part of the brain that (along with the hormone vasopressin) allows the body to regulate its water content by reducing urine output. From the hypothalamus, oxytocin travels to the posterior lobe of the pituitary gland and is released when needed.

Oxytocin and its relationship to fear, anxiety, and trust

There are oxytocin receptors in the brain of both sexes, as well as in the uterus of a pregnant woman. One of the key effects of oxytocin is to block fear, anxiety, and panic input into the amygdalae. The amygdalae is the almond-shaped group of nuclei located deep within the medial temporal lobes of the brain and is part of the limbic system, which modulates emotion, behavior, long-term memory, and olfaction.

The amygdalae is also the part of the brain that modulates trust. In effect, by blocking fear, panic, and anxiety, there can be trust. I don't think oxytocin engenders trust as much as it blocks fear, because one does not trust when one is in fear. So, it would probably be more accurate to say that oxytocin is the hormone of blocking fear rather than to call it the trust hormone. In any case, researchers have confirmed a strong link between oxytocin and sociability. In other words, when we're emotionally and physically healthy and in balance, we are naturally social.

Oxytocin and childbirth

Oxytocin is one of the primary hormones associated with childbirth. During labor, the receptor cells that allow a woman's body to respond to oxytocin are greatly increased. And it is oxytocin that stimulates powerful contractions, which helps to dilate the cervix and move the baby down and out of the birth canal. This distension of the lower birth canal and stimulation of pelvic autonomic nerves leads to oxytocin release if there is no epidural. In fact, if a woman does have an epidural she may need to be given additional oxytocin to minimize the need to use forceps.[2] Although low-dose (as opposed to high-dose) oxytocin and epidural anesthesia will increase cesarean section rates.[3] When women in labor need help to trigger or strengthen their uterine contractions, the drug they are given is called Pitocin®, which is, in fact, oxytocin.

Oxytocin in pain relief and wound healing

Oxytocin exerts an analgesic action by increasing the depolarizing action of gamma-aminobutyric acid (GABA) on the nerves that respond to pain, known as nociceptive neurons. GABA is the primary inhibitory neurotransmitter and oxytocin up regulates its action. Researchers have found that oxytocin relieves pain in newborns and makes the delivery process less problematic for the newborn.[4] And seems to be effective in relieving low back pain in children and adults as well.[5]

Oxytocin has even been shown to play a role in wound healing, which stands to reason when we connect the dots.

---

[2] http://www.ncbi.nlm.nih.gov/pubmed/6830729
[3] http://www2.cfpc.ca/local/user/files/%7B8030D89F-B698-4F9D-B6A7-190AD9866E59%7D/Kotaska%20Klein%20epidural%20oxy.pdf
[4] http://www.inmed.univ-mrs.fr/maj/upload/publications/fncel-05-00003.pdf
[5] http://journals.lww.com/spinejournal/Abstract/1994/04150/Intrathecal_Administration_of_Oxytocin_Induces.1.aspx

Understandably, when a person gets injured, stress, anxiety, and fear tend to increase. However, when we have adequate oxytocin levels, the cascade of stress hormones (primarily cortisol) is reduced and doesn't interfere with the wound healing process.[6]

Is oxytocin a mind-altering substance?

Although I have experienced the dramatic emotional impact of using oxytocin at a critical moment in my life, results aren't dramatic in every case. For example, when oxytocin is administered to an emotionally and physically healthy individual, it's likely that that person would notice minimal changes. Oxytocin does not get one "high," nor does it alter one's level of consciousness.

If you used oxytocin before going to a dinner party, would you be more outgoing and gregarious? Would you interact with greater ease and laugh more often? It could happen, but the effects would likely be rather subtle. To put it in perspective, think of a woman in labor. I, for one, have never seen a laboring mother who was given Pitocin® radically change her demeanor and ask her nurses and midwives to join hands and sing a round of Kumbaya during the birth process. But it does help her move through labor.

Oxytocin deficiency

Oxytocin receptors may decrease in a diseased or aging brain, and if receptors are destroyed or limited, such as what may happen in a child with a post-encephalitic syndrome, normal physiologic levels of oxytocin may not be enough to get done what oxytocin needs to do. Also, an injured brain may not be able to manufacture the amount of oxytocin required to

---

[6] http://www.plosone.org/article/info:doi%2F10.1371%2Fjournal.pone.0005523

do the job at hand. Using the example of a vaccine-injured child who has developed an autoimmune encephalitis, receptors on the neurons in the brain could fall victim to the attack—be they folate receptors, NMDA receptors, or—as in this example—oxytocin receptors.

There can be changes in the oxytocin levels inside the brain or cerebral spinal fluid that are independent of oxytocin levels circulating in the blood. As there isn't yet a practical way of measuring how much oxytocin is being pumped out inside the brain, one's need for oxytocin must be determined either by circumstance or empirically (by observation).

Part II

Oxytocin and Its Impact on the Maladies of Our Time

Now that you have a basic overview of the body's primary uses for oxytocin, the picture only gets more exciting from here. This subtly astounding hormone is showing great promise in treating some of our most distressing health issues, including autism, addictions, sexual dysfunction, cancer, and men's health. And, in addition to its potent applications in addressing stress, anxiety, and extreme grief, there is research indicating its efficacy in treating other mood disorders and mental health issues.

Oxytocin and autism

Although it's beyond the scope of this ebook to fully explore this complex topic, it is important to clarify that I am only using the word "autism" to provide context. As touched upon briefly in the introduction, in actuality, most children who are labeled as having "autism" have no such thing. Rather, they have an environmentally triggered immune/gastro-encephalopathy. This is a medical problem that is not being treated because it isn't being recognized by conventional medicine and is being called something it is not—it is being called autism, which is another matter entirely.

Along the spectrum of environmental encephalitic syndrome and autism, there is an increasing level of interest in oxytocin. The current medical literature indicates that children with autism have lower plasma oxytocin levels, with one of the outer expressions of this deficiency being repetitive physical behaviors, sometimes called *stimming*. One specific example of stimming is the hand flapping that can be seen in some of these children, which is actually a form of body anxiety. For several years now, I have used oxytocin as a nasal spray to successfully help ease this symptom. Since oxytocin is not treating the underlying medical problem, it should really be viewed as a Band-Aid that can support the overall healing process and improve social encounters.

Oxytocin and addiction

Simply stated, when a "like" becomes a "want" an addiction is born in the mid forebrain. This adaptive central nervous system processes actually changes the neuronal architecture, so that the nerves become physically different in the brain of an addict. This relates to alcohol addiction (opiate-ethanol interaction), cocaine addiction, and, to a lesser extent, even sugar and fat addiction. Oxytocin has been shown to inhibit the development of tolerance to morphine and to alleviate various symptoms of morphine withdrawal in mice. Tolerance to ethanol (e.g., the hypothermia-inducing effect of ethanol) also was inhibited by oxytocin.[7]

It is possible that oxytocin has the potential to reverse the physical changes that addictions can create. Experience from my own medical practice is that oxytocin alone is not enough to overcome an addiction, but in combination with a drug called baclofen, oxytocin can be very helpful.

Baclofen is an inexpensive generic drug derived from GABA that is used to treat spasticity and has been shown to reduce alcohol cravings in a double-blind study[8], as well as cigarette cravings.[9] However, baclophen suffers from the same problem that oxytocin does—there is no incentive for

[7] http://www.ncbi.nlm.nih.gov/pubmed/9924746
[8] http://alcalc.oxfordjournals.org/content/37/5/504.abstract
[9] http://www.sciencedirect.com/science/article/pii/S0376871609000957

a drug company to create a new indication for it or market it. In this context, to "market it" means educating physicians about its benefit, as well as running ads on television and radio for the general public. At the conclusion of this book, I offer information and suggestions for how physicians can effectively further the availability, use, and knowledge of oxytocin despite the lack of support from the pharmaceutical industry. Making information on oxytocin widely available could spark far-reaching support, as was the case with baclofen. An anonymous donor gave nearly one million dollars for a very large clinical trial of baclofen to commence at the University of Amersterdam in 2011. With that kind of backing, baclofen will eventually become a cornerstone treatment for addiction.

Again, given the effectiveness that I'm observing with patients when oxytocin is used in combination with baclofen, I believe there is a brighter future ahead in the field of addiction treatment.

Oxytocin and orgasm

Sexual dysfunction in women is no trivial matter, causing untold emotional stress and unnecessary self-doubt. Going through periods of time when there is difficulty reaching orgasm affects far more women than one would imagine. But this does not have to be the case. Even primary anorgasmia, which is the inability to experience orgasm, can be effectively treated with oxytocin. Temporary use of a oxytocin can rectify the problem. And while oxytocin may not address all sexual issues for all women, it is harmless to try.

Medical literature confirms that the higher the levels of oxytocin the more intense and the more frequent the orgasms.[10]

---
[10] http://www.ncbi.nlm.nih.gov/pubmed/8135652

One visible indicator of the release of oxytocin is the redness that some women have in their chest and neck area after orgasm. This "post-coital flush" happens when oxytocin causes blood vessels to dilate.

We can, again, look to women in childbirth (and even new mothers) for clues as to how oxytocin affects women in a general sense. For example, nipple stimulation is a natural way to bring about the oxytocin boost that assists with bringing on labor and lactation. In the same way, the stimulation of nipples is also an effective way to bring about orgasm, as it activates the release of oxytocin. Since some women aren't necessarily comfortable with this practice, oxytocin can be an important part of the tool kit for jump-starting the desired process.

Oxytocin also lowers blood pressure, which is why physicians who use Pitocin® with their laboring mothers know to watch out for hypotension (low blood pressure) after a bolus of this form of IV oxytocin is administered. In men, this drop in blood pressure could also explain, in part, why they feel like falling asleep after an orgasm.

An important side note: Speaking of sleep, many people use the hormone melatonin to fall asleep at night, but it should be pointed out that melatonin seems to block the action of oxytocin.[11]

Further sexual healing - *a personal note*

I once watched a fascinating documentary that included interviews with men who had survived Nazi torture. One of the gentlemen talked about how he would think of his sexual exploits while he was being tortured; it was a mind trick he employed to make the horrors he was experiencing more

[11] http://ebm.rsmjournals.com/cgi/content/abstract/138/3/1002

tolerable. Fortunately for this particular man, he had a vast library of past sexual encounters to pull from. I remember thinking that his pleasurable memories would have caused his brain to release oxytocin, which would, in turn, minimize the amount of fear and panic that anyone would naturally experience under those unimaginable circumstances. And given the analgesic effects of oxytocin, it's probable that his memories reduced the actual physical pain he was feeling as well.

About one month after my son passed, it turned out that the remembrance of this documentary served me well. It wasn't until that point that I had a thought that could be considered even remotely sexual—but a small thought did arrive, like a nearly imperceptible breeze. And in that fleeting moment, I noticed that the intense level of grief, which had been my constant companion, modulated ever so slightly. It was at that very moment that I thought about the TV documentary I had seen almost a year earlier—and I remembered oxytocin. Within a couple of days, I had oxytocin nasal spray in my hands and began to use it with dramatic results.

Oxytocin and cancer

This is the point in this brief tale of healing possibilities where the story of oxytocin gets even more interesting. Research is showing that cancer cells that have oxytocin receptors because they came from organs that have those receptors, such as breast tissue, show a decrease in cancer cell growth if exposed to oxytocin.[12]

This bears repeating: In tumors, oxytocin acts as a growth regulator through the activation of what is called a *G-coupled transmembrane receptor*, the oxytocin receptor. There seems to be one notable exception to this protective effect of oxy-

---

[12] http://cat.inist.fr/?aModele=afficheN&cpsidt=15707703

tocin on cancer cell proliferation and that has to do with the prostate.[13] A study published in the journal *Lancet* reviewed data from 47 epidemiological studies in 30 countries and has clearly confirmed that breastfeeding lowers breast cancer risk substantially.[14] The relative risk of breast cancer is reduced by 4.3 per cent for each year that a woman breastfeeds, in addition to a reduction of 7 per cent for each birth. On top of all the oxytocin that is released during the birth process, the infant's suckling keeps the mother's oxytocin levels high.

Women without children can mimic this benefit through the nipple stimulation that I addressed above, but doing this consistently can be challenging. The use of oxytocin would probably stand a better chance of delivering a consistent and regular dose of this healing hormone.

Oxytocin and men's health

Good news: Men are not left out of the potential benefit of oxytocin. Even looking back to my first year in medical school, I am reminded of its benefits. Not surprisingly, I found myself stressed and depressed more than I care to remember. I had no social life to speak of, which, of course, only exacerbated the stress. Then a lovely medical student from England came to visit the school I was attending, and I fell head over heels for her. Immediately, I noticed physiological and emotional changes. For one thing, I must have been suffering from low testosterone despite my young age, because I noticed my beard started growing in faster. Just the presence of the female of the species will increase oxytocin levels in the male of the species[15]—and oxytocin itself in-

[13] http://www.mendeley.com/research/oxytocin-induces-the-migration-of-prostate-cancer-cells-involvement-of-the-gicoupled-signaling-pathway/#
[14] http://www.ncbi.nlm.nih.gov/pubmed/12133652
[15] http://www.scielo.cl/scielo.php?pid=S0716-97602006000200007&script=sci_arttext

creases testosterone production.[16] Of course, wild infatuation isn't a necessity—there are natural lifestyle choices that will increase oxytocin in men—but there are times when it's just what the doctor ordered.

With years of professional and personal experience since those early days in med school, I will be the first to acknowledge that oxytocin alone will not cause people to fall in love or facilitate long-lasting relationships. However, it can help a great deal in certain situations and can even be a lifesaver. I have worked with men who couldn't ejaculate due to taking antidepressants (which can block the action of oxytocin) but were able to fully regain their sexual function by using oxytocin. As described earlier, I have also worked with anorgasmic women who were able to breakthrough their invisible blockages; women who had all but given up on their ability to have intense sexual pleasure were able to easily achieve orgasm. These are vitally important improvements in an individual's life and, as I tell my patients, sometimes cannot be accomplished by simply singing happy songs or taking a walk in the woods…unless one takes oxytocin along.

Ultimately, what I tell all of my male patients is this: Don't take oxytocin if you don't really need it, just like you shouldn't take any other hormone or drug indiscriminately. There is some evidence that oxytocin increases prostatic hypertrophy[17] and could increase the possibility of prostate cancer metastases.[18] So, there is risk as well as benefit, which is why the use of oxytocin should be done under a physician's supervision, especially if it is used regularly for a prolonged period of time.

An important side note: It is of interest that the hormone melatonin, mentioned earlier for interfering with

---

[16] http://www.biolreprod.org/content/52/6/1268.short
[17] http://www.ncbi.nlm.nih.gov/pubmed/8714010
[18] http://www.ncbi.nlm.nih.gov/pubmed/20663860

the action of oxytocin, has been found to reduce prostate cancer cell growth.[19]

---

[19] http://www.ncbi.nlm.nih.gov/pubmed/15378522

Part III

Oxytocin – Sources and Dosage

Where to get oxytocin

First, a refresher on key measurement abbreviations:

ml = milliliters
IU = international units

Any physician can prescribe oxytocin to any pharmacy. What the pharmacy will order is a box of twelve 10 ml vials of 10 IU/ml. Most pharmacies will not want to place this order unless the ordering physician can assure them he will eventually put in enough prescriptions to use up that supply. That might intimidate a physician ordering oxytocin for the first time. The safest route is to contact a compounding pharmacy to create a nasal spray or make the tablets for sublingual use.

While not all compounding pharmacies will fill an oxytocin prescription, the vast majority will. Although you can use the compounding pharmacy of your choice, here is a brief resource directory that may be useful to you and your doctor:

www.womensinternational.com
Women's International Pharmacy
2 March Court Madison WI
Tel: (800) 699-8144

www.BelmarPharmacy.com
Belmar Pharmacy 12860 W Cedar Dr #210
Lakewood, CO 80228
Tel: (800) 525-9473

www.austincompounding.com
Specialty Compounding
211 S Bell
Cedar Park, TX 78613
Tel: (877) 287-8679

www.menaulcompoundingpharmacy.com
Menaul Compounding Pharmacy
11417 Menaul Boulevard Northeast
Albuquerque, NM 87112-1794
Tel: (505) 291-1600

www.fusionrxcompounding.com
Fusion Rx Compounding
3679 Motor Ave Ste 305
Los Angeles CA 90034
Tel: (888) 792 6676

www.collegepharmacy.com
College Pharmacy
3505 Austin Bluffs Parkway
Colorado Springs, CO 80918
Tel: (800) 888-9358 or (719) 262-0022

www.wellnesshealth.com
Wellness Pharmacy
3401 Independence Drive, Suite 231
Birmingham, Alabama 35209
Tel: (800) 227-2627

www.hopewellrx.com
Hopewell Pharmacy
1 West Broad Street
Hopewell, NJ 08525-1999
Tel: (609) 466-1960

Oxytocin dosing

At this time, there are not a lot of dosing studies in the medical literature, especially not for the more cutting-edge applications of oxytocin. But it is notable that for the purpose of helping breastfeeding, the dose of 100 IU (taken as a sublingual tablet) was only slightly more effective than the lower dose of 10 IU.

As outlined above, the oxytocin that a regular pharmacy would order comes in vials of 10 IU per ml and each vial is 10 ml. **That said, 1 ml of that vial turned into nasal drops would be a safe starting place for any condition.**

When I was using oxytocin to help navigate my grief, I used 40 to 50 IU/ml compounded as a nasal spray, and most nasal pumps typically put out 0.1 ml per squirt, so each squirt may be 5 IU maximum. There are only so many oxytocin receptors in the brain and, while they only stay saturated for a finite period of time, I would not use oxytocin more than four times a day for most indications.

Oxytocin is not physiologically addicting, but it can be psychologically addicting. With that understanding, know that using oxytocin more than four times a day will only make the pharmacy happier—but not necessarily you.

Consulting with Dr. Stoller

As stated in the introduction, my primary intention in writing this booklet is to empower those who need oxytocin with information and resources that will help them to obtain a prescription if needed. In discussing oxytocin with your physician or nurse practitioner, you can also use this booklet as a reference guide, to answer questions that might arise if they aren't already familiar with its expanded uses.

If you need additional support and wish to contact me directly, the following two categories describe my availability:

For patients in New Mexico and California
I am available for in-person consultations and tele-medicine sessions via Skype and can prescribe oxytocin.

For patients with urgent needs outside of New Mexico and California, I am available to consult with patients (or their families) and to interface with their physicians or other licensed healthcare practitioners. Once a consultation is complete, I provide the necessary letter via fax or email for the healthcare giver who will be prescribing the oxytocin.

Contact me via email: info@griefsos.com

Conclusion

A Message of Empowerment

Since my goal is to help alleviate the physical, emotional, and mental suffering of people everywhere, I wish to conclude with a few words that will clarify not only some of the obstacles that we face regarding the study and availability of oxytocin, but—even more importantly—some of the ways that both physicians and laypeople can work toward removing those obstacles.

It's probably of little surprise to know that drugs or medical devices will not become part of standard medical care unless there is someone or some corporation making a lot of money marketing it. And a lot of drugs and vaccines become accepted as part of standard medical care not because they are actually efficacious or even safe, but—again—because there is a lot of money to be made in promoting that new drug or vaccine. There is actually a term for drugs that remain commercially undeveloped owing to limited potential for profitability—they are called orphan drugs. And with the exception of its use in the delivery room, oxytocin fits into this category.

Translational medicine

Now, we are not completely at the mercy of drug companies or their profit motive. The missing link for orphan drugs is something called translational medicine. Translational medicine studies examine and track results of interventions in the real world. It is part of evidence-based medicine that should take place after a blinded randomized controlled trial (RCT) but is usually an ignored part of evidence-based medicine instead. Just doing RCTs (which are often done over and over) will not make an "orphan therapy" part of standard of care, but—as the name implies—a translational medical study will!

Treatment registries for launching translational medical studies

Beyond its tremendous aid to people dealing with toxic levels of stress, anxiety, panic, fear, and grief, oxytocin also appears to benefit individuals with various forms of mental illness. For example, there is compelling pilot study data in humans showing that oxytocin can relieve the symptoms of schizophrenia[20]. The problem, as stated above, is that this will not become standard medical practice unless a drug company sees great potential to market oxytocin specifically for treating schizophrenia and invests large amounts of resources in clinical trials and the drug application process.

But why would a drug company do this when everyone knows that oxytocin can be obtained generically? Well, they won't do it…they have zero incentive to do anything. However, there is a way to bypass drug companies and still make something standard of care. There are entities called Treatment Registries where physicians can launch translational medical studies. One such notable registry is the John Eisenberg Treatment Registry at Oklahoma University (http://treatmentregistry.org). Under the watchful supervision of a governing university, a translational medical study can demonstrate that the orphan drug, such as oxytocin, is efficacious in treating any given condition in the real world, because a translational study tracks real results. Although the study won't change the FDA label for that drug (because that is a matter between

---

[20] http://rengou.w3.kanazawa-u.ac.jp/shiminhiroba/Adjunctive.pdf

the FDA and the manufacturer), it can allow that drug to gain recognition as a *reimbursable therapy* that has merit and thus becomes standard of care.

Endnotes

1. http://www.youtube.com/watch?v=BEAgT91XV5A&feature=related
2. http://www.ncbi.nlm.nih.gov/pubmed/6830729
3. http://www2.cfpc.ca/local/user/files/%7B8030D89F-B698-4F9D-B6A7-190AD9866E59%7D/Kotaska%20Klein%20epidural%20oxy.pdf
4. http://www.inmed.univ-mrs.fr/maj/upload/publications/fncel-05-00003.pdf
5. http://journals.lww.com/spinejournal/Abstract/1994/04150/Intrathecal_Administration_of_Oxytocin_Induces.1.aspx
6. http://www.plosone.org/article/info:doi%2F10.1371%2Fjournal.pone.0005523
7. http://www.ncbi.nlm.nih.gov/pubmed/9924746
8. http://alcalc.oxfordjournals.org/content/37/5/504.abstract
9. http://www.sciencedirect.com/science/article/pii/S0376871609000957
10. http://www.ncbi.nlm.nih.gov/pubmed/8135652
11. http://ebm.rsmjournals.com/cgi/content/abstract/138/3/1002
12. http://cat.inist.fr/?aModele=afficheN&cpsidt=15707703
13. http://www.mendeley.com/research/oxytocin-induces-the-migration-of-prostate-cancer-cells-involvement-of-the-gicoupled-signaling-pathway/#
14. http://www.ncbi.nlm.nih.gov/pubmed/12133652
15. http://www.scielo.cl/scielo.php?pid=S0716-97602006000200007&script=sci_arttext
16. http://www.biolreprod.org/content/52/6/1268.short

17. http://www.ncbi.nlm.nih.gov/pubmed/8714010
18. http://www.ncbi.nlm.nih.gov/pubmed/20663860
19. http://www.ncbi.nlm.nih.gov/pubmed/15378522
20. http://rengou.w3.kanazawa-u.ac.jp/shiminhiroba/Adjunctive.pdf

Please visit these other notable sites created by Dr. Stoller.

http://www.hbotnm.com
http://www.sfhbo.com
http://www.BodiesinRebellion.com
http://www.GriefSOS.com
http://www.autismclock.com
http://www.dreamtreaderpress.com

Hope for the Future

It is my sincere hope that this book will help advance an understanding of how oxytocin can be used for several "orphan" indications, especially acute grief. As I have stated throughout, knowledge of this powerhouse hormone needs to come to the fore to alleviate many areas of unnecessary suffering.

It's my belief that when life shows you something that could benefit a great many, there is a responsibility that goes with that—to help spread the word. May this information serve you, your loved ones, and your friends for the rest of your lives, bringing increased health, happiness, and peace.

About K Paul Stoller, MD, FACHM

K Paul Stoller, MD, started his medical career as a pediatrician and was a Diplomat of the American Board of Pediatrics for over two decades. Previously, in the early 1970s, he was a University of California President's Undergraduate Fellow in the Health Sciences, working in the UCLA Department of Anesthesiology and volunteering at the since disbanded Parapsychology Lab at the UCLA Neuro Psychiatric Institute. He matriculated at Penn State, and then completed his postgraduate training at UCLA.

His first published works, papers on psychopharmacology, came to print before he entered medical school. During medical school, he was hired to do research for the Humane Society of the United States, and became involved in an effort to prohibit the use of shelter dogs for medical experiments, which made himself very unpopular in certain circles when he published an article entitled "Sewer Science and Pound Seizure" in the *International Journal for the Study of Animal Problems*. He was then invited and became a founding board member of the Humane Farming Association, and served as science editor for *The Animals Voice Magazine* where he was nominated for a Maggie award.

In the mid 1990's, after a friend, head of Apple Computer's Advanced Technology Group, lapsed into a coma, Dr. Stoller began investigating hyperbaric medicine. Soon after, he started administering hyperbaric oxygen to brain-injured children and adults, including Iraqi vets and retired NFL players with traumatic brain injuries, also pioneering the use of this therapy for treating children with fetal alcohol syndrome. He is a Fellow of the American College of Hyperbaric Medicine and has served as president of the International Hyperbaric Medical Association for almost a decade.

When his son was killed in a train accident in 2007, he discovered the effectiveness of the hormone oxytocin in treating pathological grief. Dr. Stoller has medical offices in Santa Fe, Sacramento, and San Francisco.

Made in United States
North Haven, CT
14 July 2024